On a blue-dazzle April day

On a blue-dazzle April day

Poems 1938 - 1993

Elizabeth Smith-Wright

SMH BOOKS

British Library Cataloguing in Publication Data

A catalogue record for this book is available from the
British Library.

ISBN paperback 0 9512619 5 9

First published April 1994 by
SMH BOOKS
Pear Tree Cottage, Watersfield, Pulborough
West Sussex, RH20 lNG

Typeset by
INKWELL, Cocking, West Sussex

Bookcover design by Sandra Saer
Cover photograph taken at LEONARDSLEE GARDENS
Lower Beeding, Sussex
by Keith Harding, Goodness Gracious

Printed and bound in Great Britain by
Hillman Printers (Frome) Ltd.

To my dear twin, Jill,
without whom
life would not have been
half so much fun.

CONTENTS

11

On a blue-dazzle April day

Here I am, walking in spring
On a blue-dazzle April day
In my seventy-fifth year.

The breeze ruffles the blossom
Of cherry and magnolia.
What does it whisper to me?
"Make the most of this beauty",
It says. "There cannot be
Many more Aprils for you.
Make the most of this day
Because, in the nature of things,
It could be your last...

April, 1993

Extract from 'The Little Boatman'

So swiftly and softly I worked on the desolate room
To make it more worthy of you when you should awake.
I flung wide the windows to let in the sweet river-breeze;
The sunlight came streaming all over the floors;
Cuckoo-song, echoes of cuckoo-song, came to my ears
That had heard nothing so sweet as the voice of a bird
Since he, whom I loved more than my life,was gone,
Drifting down the river for home...
I searched in the tangle of weeds that once was my garden,
and found
windflowers growing, and primroses starring the ground.
Gathering only the loveliest blossoms, I brought them to you
So when you awoke, my room was alive with the
rapture of spring.

1938

The Comrade

I have not seen you with these mortal eyes and yet
If you should pass me in the crowded street
One in a throng of thousands, I should know your face
And I would not pass by unrecognised.
Time is of no account; it does not matter when
Or in what unfamiliar place
The solitary journey ends and we, the travellers, meet.
I am contented, since so long ago I realised
In some miraculous way
That you, beloved Stranger, are aware of me...

I have not heard your voice except in memory,
And yet the voices that I know in daily speech
Are not more real to me and never were so dear.
You have made solitude and silence sweet
Though the whole world be shouting, I am deaf,
Though you but whisper in my sleeping brain, I hear.
So when the moment comes and we, half frightened,
Clinging each to each, dare not believe our eyes,
Will know the miracle complete,
Hearing the broken welcome on the other's lips:
"My love.. my Comrade.. it is I..."

1939

Reverie
(to J.S.E.)

Snow drifting in silence through streets of an ancient town;
Footfalls of passers-by and voices heard for a while
Then lost in the darkening air... and who shall say
How many feet have passed this way since time began,
How many voices called?

Who shall know of the eyes that watched the falling snow
On countless winter afternoons so long ago? The ears
That listened to other feet walking with steady step and heard
Some other voice call down the echoing street?

Were those eyes brilliant with life, or misted with thought,
Filled with a wild unrest, or dark with pain?
What did they see in the wintry afternoon?

But that was Yesterday... and who can tell of these things?
Who can say how it was?

1940

Poem

This was the time of day we loved the best:
A quiet dusk after the summer heat was gone;
Sunset a glowing memory in the west
And one faint star that trembled as it shone.

Still blows the breeze, the same star's shining still,
The same enchanted silence falls, as when
I stood beside the gate, waiting until
I heard your footsteps echo in the quiet lane.

You will not come again, though I should wait
Dusk after summer dusk, nor shall I receive
Your kiss - pledge of our friendship, at the gate,
Nor hear you speak my name...I do not grieve.

In all my memories of you, grief has no part.
I know Time cannot steal, nor death destroy
The love that is between us, and my heart
Remembers you this night and always with a joy

Deeper than words can say. Through you I knew
How lovely life could be...Such rare and fine
Treasures do I possess - because of you,
Humour and courage and a lasting peace are mine.

The twilight deepens, dew is on the grass and soon
The sky is sown with stars and all those trees
Break into silver blossom under the rising moon;
The garden sleeps and softly dies the breeze.

O friend and lover of the years gone by, it seems
Tonight but a moment since you went away -
The slow and empty years between but dreams,
The last time you smiled at me was yesterday.

1940

The Children
(to A.A.)

"It's growing cold", said one, turning away. "Call them to bed!"
I remember you gazing across the darkening field, your eyes
Filled with a sad compassion, as you said,
"Ah, let them play..." and the air resounded with their sweet,
    wild cries.

Moved by a strange delight, born of the April dusk, they leapt
Dancing over the grass among the dew;
Lost for a while was grim reality, and terror slept,
Time paused, and the world stood still, for you.

Then gently you called the children away, and following after,
A cold, unfriendly wind hurried over the field,
Chilled us all to the bone, and hushed our laughter;
And terror woke, as the first faint sirens wailed.

Dark is the present, darkness all that the years may bring.
But we will remember, when everything else is a dream,
How happiness wrapped us about for one brief moment,
In a field, one far-off evening in spring.

Surrey, 1941

Thoughts on watching the sunset

O bare, black boughs against the pallid glow of sunset;
O pale clouds anchored in the pale March sky;
Evening of serenity and calm fade not too swiftly,
For with your dying, others also die.

O dusk, approach not yet: for with your stealthy footfall
Gone is the day's security, and fled
The pearly calm of clouds; and gone, the golden-peaceful
Hour of sunset. Silence, too is dead.

For, with the darkness, all the air's alive with secret clamour:
The dreadful humming that precedes the storm.
Upon the sky's dark face a thousand livid scars of searchlights
Blaze... and the world is trembling with alarm.

So when tonight the watchful siren's cry breaks through our
     dreaming,
When brave hearts fail, and fearfully comes the breath,
Only our desperate belief in that same sun's returning
Stands between us and sudden, whistling death.

1942

Extract from 'Lost Way'
(to D.H.)

O you who loved and lost me, seek again!
Deep in the woods of Spring pursue the soul of me
Down sunlit glades, up undulating hills
Through star-bright streams and meadows sweet with rain.
Dear friend, if you would find the whole of me,
Look for my heart among the daffodils.

1943

To M.B.

Driven by fear, I sought for shelter at your door.
You did not hesitate nor ask why I had come,
You offered me, until my hurt was healed,
A haven and a home.

Now when my Enemy at nightfall comes for me,
Breaks through the gate that all day long I have patrolled,
Yours is the voice that answers when I call
And yours the hand I hold.

When morning breaks, I dare not think of you,
But set my will against my memory, to prove
I still am master in my mind, for I
Am haunted now by love.

Vainly I wander through the woods and flowered fields.
Their life and loveliness, my eyes beguile.
Still etched in beauty on my mind, I see
Your wise and tender smile.
I would escape this bondage of the heart, and seek
Far, among strangers, the peace of mind I lost;
And through time's alchemy you might become
A long-forgotten ghost.

But neither time nor distance can avail me now;
I am outrun, outwitted, even if I knew
In which direction I should turn my steps,
For all roads lead to you.

1947

The house they never left
(Land army - Chichester)

Come with me down a certain street when dusk is falling,
An April dusk that fills the heart with a nameless ache.
(When will Time's kindly hand obliterate this place,
Or Memory release its ruthless hold?).

Pause at this house with the sentinel street lamp shining
Outside the gate. No living thing within these walls,
But dust and silence, and the gathering gloom. (And yet
Peace resides not here, nor sleep.)

Come with me up the darkening stair, and harken
At this open door - only a glimmering floor and bare walls.
But surely you feel the sorrow in this room, the sense of pain?
(It weighs me down whenever I come back...)

Step inside under the eaves, for here is joy -
It sings in the very air, a joy that will not be denied,
Piercingly young, and unaware of death. (So very hard to bear:
I see you feel it, too, my friend.)

Lean on the sill a moment; breath deeply of the spring.
The breeze is stirring in the sycamore tree. Listen again...
Are you sure it is the breeze you hear?
(A sigh might sound like that,
Or laughter muted by the passing years...)

Close the door quietly, come away, down these shadowy stairs.
(Do not look back, my friend, I beg you.)
Let us seek warmth and light where you may stay - but I?
Only till Memory drags me back again...

Chichester
December, 1947

Tomorrow's dusk

I am not lonely when the sun goes down. From dawn,
Through countless mornings, endless afternoons, I work
Till daylight dies. Then with the dusk I go
On secret paths of thought, to that dear house which stands
Somewhere between the sunset and the alien night.

The traffic's hum, the cries below me in the street,
Loosen their hold upon me; I am free. The fields
Take shape beneath my eager gaze and every tree
Shifts into focus, till the whole loved landscape lies
Framed in the window where I wait - where I have been
Waiting for you, since I was young.

I will not fail you, friend. I will keep tryst, though now
The years are passing and my tired eyes
Grow dim with staring out across the shadowed fields.
So many times I thought I saw you, thought I heard
The voice I knew, calling a long way off...
Always the figure dwindled on the darkening hill;
Always the voice became the cry of some wild bird.

Sometimes when darkness falls, and silence, as I lie
Lie without sleep or comfort, there arrives a deep despair,
Seizing my heart with panic fingers; and it seems
Past all belief that you should ever come. The dream
That has illumined all my life may play me false
And dusk will fall, forever bringing only night.

O heart, be strong, be steadfast! Only so can I
Live out my days in patience, true to my belief
That on some quiet evening, lovelier than most,
Footsteps will cross the field, a lantern shine
With a clear and gathering radiance that proclaims
The long, long watch is over and my heart's at peace
Knowing that you have come at last to call me home.

1948

To my Mother on her Birthday

Do not be sad, dear heart, though you were lovely then,
Though youth's brief springtime comes no more for you.
Time has not dimmed your radiance, nor pain contrived
To still your laughter or your heart subdue.

You are more lovely *now*. In your sweet face, the years
Have marked their passing with such tenderness
That God, the source of beauty, will be proud to make
Part of his heaven from your loveliness.

1948

Fear and the pit and the snare...

"Fear and the pit and the snare, shall be upon you O inhabitant of the earth... The moon shall be confounded and the sun ashamed."
(Isaiah 24:17, 23)

Over there, in the corner, where moonlight and shadows mingle,
I see two eyes.
They are dark, and fierce and afraid behind their tangle of hair.
I see a body outlined with crude crouching limbs, and a hand
More like a paw, that clutches a glimmering flint.
He watches me, turning his hairy head as I move.
(I know who he was; I know who he will be.)

I feel no fear in his presence because I can look in his brain;
I know how he thinks; I can feel his sensations; I know
Why he snarls, why he cowers and trembles, and clutches his flint
Bewildered and lost in an anguish of horror...

He is seeing, in me, the product of thousands of years
Of growth and development, progress and knowledge.
He is looking at me through an infinite darkness of Time;
He is seeing - himself.

No, I am not afraid of him, poor Ape-man,
Crouched in the shadows, his dull brain darkened
With the horror of what the future holds...
I feel no fear in his presence,
Just a tremendous shame.

1948

"Peradventure He sleepeth"

...But when God wakes - ah, when He wakes, what then?
As some day from his age-long slumber roused,
He climbs to wakefulness out of the mists of time,
What will become of us, poor shadow-men, and that
Great whirling sphere that was our home?

Shall we dissolve as pictures in the brain,
As though we had not been... our shattered earth
Gone without trace into the limbo of forgotten things?
Or will we lie weeping in darkness, lost beyond hope of birth
While centuries away our universe
Spins on in desolation?

Perhaps we shall sink into oblivion's kindly arms;
The world will cease to turn, hanging in outer space
Amid the silence of a great despair,
Waiting for God to dream us all again.

1948

To M.B.
(Died 1949)

A child, I looked for you in candlelight
And when the dying fire threw shadows round my bed,
voiceless I called
And motionless I fought the rising tide of terror
Till I reached your hand: my talisman against the night.
Over the borderline of sleep you always slipped away.
I never saw your face.

I looked for you in Autumn, when the morning mist
Lay on the fields and all the woods were still.
In that great hush I might have heard you call from the
dreaming hill.
But sunrise came and all the birds were singing, and my eyes,
Dazzled by so much splendour, filled with tears.

Lost in a midnight town I looked for you
Down snowy streets and strange, lit by a spangle of lamps
Dwindling away to a blur against the black
Of the sullen winter sky. And further off
The timeless twinkle of stars.
But morning found me sleeping.
I had not reached the end of the road.

I looked for you when every Spring came round.
I watched the dusk through a glimmering roof of blossom,
Reaching out in my mind to things as yet unknown...

1949
(Unfinished)

When I die

I do not wish for human immortality.
When this warm flesh lies cold, this beating heart is still.
I have endured too much of self. Then, I would be
Part of the silence on the evening hill.

Let those who hope to pass on to some higher plane
Strive for their heaven, and the best they may become.
Let me have peace; condemn me not to feel again
This endless longing of the heart for home.

Some say that we, released by death, no longer blind,
Shall see all beauty at the Source and worship there.
Then let me be forever sightless, since I find
The lesser loveliness of earth too much to bear.

To those who think we sleep awhile and then return
To this same struggling star, give them their hearts' desire.
But when my wild and wayward flame has ceased to burn,
Light of the World, re-kindle not the fire.

Or if Thy Law forbids that any thing should be
Lost in complete oblivion, let me when I die,
Become a part of all that I have loved - the sea,
Starlight and springtime and the morning sky.

Wimpole Teachers' Training College
1949

Spellbound

I sat next to a witch on the bus tonight. Her dress
Was dark as the ivy that grows on the churchyard wall,
And her hair
Gleamed deadly as berries of nightshade against her cheek.
Did nobody see her but I? Did nobody guess?
Did nobody notice at all
The thrice the conductor had stooped to ask for her fare?
The breath died in my throat with longing to hear her speak,
But she made
Never a sound save the clink of the coins as she paid.
I think the conductor knew that something was strange,
For his face was white when he handed her back her change.

I sat there, still as a stone, and after a while
She turned and looked at me, hunched at her side in a trance.
And her eyes
Were gold as an adder's. My heart leapt out of my breast
At the sight of that face, with its sidelong, secretive smile.
The beautiful, glittering glance.

Then came the terminus. Passengers started to rise.
I watched as she rose with the rest
And was gone,
Leaving me here in the darkness, bereft and forlorn.

Hours have passed, yet I crouch here, unable to move,
And weep for a witch, for love of a witch, for love...

1st prize, Chichester Arts Festival
1956

The Wood that has no name

When I was young, I shut my heart away
From human love, and turned a cheek of stone
To the kiss of friendship. Proud, I would not play
But wandered, discontented, all alone.
And so one April day
I came to the Wood that has no name, no name.

A strange, still Wood, a waiting Wood
It seemed to me; but even as I stood
Half in the morning sunshine, half in the green
And glimmering twilight under the trees, between
Me and the sun a shadow fell, a cloud
Risen from nowhere, chilling the April air.
And deep in my brain a whisper, sharp and loud,
Kept on and on: "Beware! beware! beware!"

I wavered there at the edge of the Wood, my gaze
Still on the darkening sky, and then - I heard
The singing; my chance was gone. I knew no bird
Had ever sung like that... each crystal phrase
Rippling the silence like a pebble thrown
Into still water, called to my heart alone.
I realised, beyond all certainty
That the Singer sang for me, for me.

I turned my back on the sky and swiftly stepped
Into the Wood, nor paused to mark the place
Where I went in. How often have I wept
For that far morning! Could I but retrace
My steps and find again the gap in the trees
And glimpse the sky and feel the vigorous breeze,
Listen to human speech and hold
A hand that is warm not cold, not cold...

But all I see is the glimmering green and all
I hear is the song; the song that never ends.
I cannot drown it even when I call
The boys and girls who would have been my friends.
O, desperately I call you! Search for me
As long ago in hide-and-seek you sought
Each other till the sun went down, and caught
The last wild straggler as he fled for Home!

Vainly I call, for you can never come
Who have been dead and gone a century.
You all reached Home, but I, who spurned the game,
Am lost in the Wood,
the Wood that has no name.

1958

Cynic at sunrise

Once when I could not sleep, I wandered out
As day was breaking on the hill, and saw a child
Who leapt and tumbled in the dew, his limbs
Like the bare branches of some ivory tree - a tree
Too frail to bear the weight of blossomed boughs.
Clad in the beauty of his nakedness, he ran
And caught the shimmering morning in his arms.

Deeper and brighter burned the amazing gold,
Until the very air seemed flushed; the boy
Flung up his arms, and turned towards the east.
I stared, half-mocking, at the enchanted child - until
I saw his face.
When I am old and spent,
Please God, may I remember how I stood, ashamed,
Pierced to the heart by that adoring gaze.

1959

Child of Adam

I was never told the tale of the flaming sword.
I did not know that, to all the children of Earth,
Eden is out of bounds.

Some day, I was sure. I would hear the words of the song;
Discover the flower that grew for me alone,
And find the longed-for friend.
Some day I would trace the stream to its sparkling source,
(If I drank of the spring where it welled from the secret place,
I knew I should never grow old.)

But no one told me the song is a song without words;
That the flower, when found, holds poison in its cup
Which sends the finder mad;
That I would not see the friend this side of dream,
For that face, serene as the peace of God, was the face
Of man before the Fall.

And of any who found the source of the stream, not one
Returned to warn me, that if I drank of the spring,
I would not live to grow old.

1960

A Song for tomorrow

"Eat, drink and be merry", so they said
A long time since, before Hiroshima. They said
"Tomorrow we shall die". And so they did.

And so shall we. Eat, then, the lifeless bread;
Drink of the water, poisoned at the source;
Drown you in wine, or feast till Kingdom Come -
It makes no odds: we all shall die the death.

Tomorrow we shall die. Today the rain
Carries the fall-out from the mushroom cloud
Over the meadows where the lovers lie.

Along the Vietnam road, towards us, runs the child
Naked, burnt to the bone. She runs
For ever and for ever, and her face
Torments our dreams and shadows every dawn.

Tomorrow we shall die. But long ago
We died in Belsen, and in Buchenwald.
We die behind the Berlin Wall, we die
In Ulster by the assassin's hand, that yesterday
Placed hands devoutly round a rosary.

Be merry - if you can. Aye, there's the rub.
Again the casual voice across the listening air:
"A bomb was planted in the town last night" -
Was planted, ripened in the dark and burst
In flame and anguish on the innocent.
Laugh if you will, but only if the head
That wears a diadem of splintered glass, is yours.

Smile, while the suckling seal drops its slow tears,
The brightness of the tiger burns away.
Mock at the pinch of rainbow dust that marks
Where the last Swallowtail's corroded wings
Conceded victory to the alien air. Make jest
Where, desperate in enormous grief, the whale
Dives in his death-throes deep through scarlet seas.

O lovely, lovely Earth... We, who have ravaged you,
Seek no forgiveness for the unforgivable.
Tomorrow we shall die. When that tomorrow comes
May we, who proved unworthy of our life,
Even at this late hour, deserve our death.

1960

The Punishment

I saw a goblin in the wood at dusk.
I set a trap to catch him, then I hid
Deep in a flowering bush and lay in wait,
Hoping my trap would hold him, and it did.

Excitedly, I left my hiding place
To watch him struggle in the darkening air.
He cried a little when I cut the wire
That held his fragile, captive body there.

I gripped him in my hand and shone a torch
Cruelly into his primrose face. His lip
Curled and he sparkled hate from topaz eyes,
But his heart fluttered against my finger-tips.

Merciless, gloating, I began to run,
Dodging among the trees in the nightfall wood.
That alien heartbeat, thrilling through my hand,
Kindled a kind of madness in the blood.

I came at last where moonlight made my eyes
Mistake the homeward road for somewhere strange;
Far off, a clock struck midnight, and I paused,
Bewildered while the world began to change.

Where was the old tree stump, the farmyard gate?
What was that shimmering there, where the gate should be?
Where was the wood I had just come through, and why
Did I feel the wind blow cold, so suddenly?

I held my hand to the moonlight, though I knew,
I knew he was gone, that only a withered leaf,
Lay in my palm; and in my breast, a heart
Past loving, past remorse, past joy, past grief.

I hold my hand to the moonlight... but I know
Nothing do I possess, nor ever will.
The homeward road leads nowhere and the wind
Sighs in an empty sky, and time stands still.

1960

Swan on the estuary

Beautiful, beautiful swan ...
Sail like a small and shining ship,
With your black webs oaring the water at your side,
Curve your snowy serpentine neck in pride,
Rocking alone on the wind-blown autumn tide.

Beautiful beautiful swan ...
Arch your wings, and show me the sudden depth
Of incredible feathery white that lies between,
So white, in the hollow there, it is palest green,
So white, that I long to be tiny, like Thumbeline

And bury myself so deep, so deep,
In that lovely hollow and sleep and sleep,
Cradled in arch-angelic peace,
Where silence is, and I might cease
From being me. O let me go,
Rocking to sleep in a dream of snow.

Beautiful, beautiful swan...

1961

To F.B.E.
(1958-1978)

The path I followed from birth led downward,
Skirted precipices, wound through tunnels -
Tunnels where daylight beckoned in vain the other end,
For when I reached the end it was always night.

And then, at last the path came to the caves,
The innermost caves of non-reality.
As cavern opened on cavern, I called on God,
And He, in His infinite mercy, sent you to me.

Hands stretched out in the dark,
Warmth in the frozen air;
Footsteps where silence was,
Lamp lit for the lost.

The path still winds, but upward now.
If you go on ahead, I will follow, without fear.
I have climbed above the mist high enough,
To see the morning star.

By nightfall, because I love you, I shall reach home.

1961

In Memoriam (T.C.)

I had thought, when your coffin began to move
And the first impulse to go with it had given way
To stillness and the refusal to watch - I had thought
That would be all, except perhaps, the first
Impression of empty rooms; but that would pass -
One can get used to anything, so they say.

I reckoned without you, my dear.
When the funeral was over
And the secret tears had dried,
I was eager to get home, to tell you all about it,
You were always ready to listen
I can hear you now...
"Start at the beginning, and tell me everything!"
But I should have had to start at the end.

The grip of your hand that last time, holding mine,
Told me what I have always known - the knowledge
I used to weep for when I was young -
That you were not a suitable candidate for death,
Nor I, for sorrow.

1961

Evening journey by train

Peach and primrose, turquoise and lavender.
Grey smudges of purple and bronze -
Sunset in early November.

The train jogs past a quiet lake
Ringed in its darkling trees;
Fading, the rose and the gold
Reflect in the sleeping water.

Something tugs at my heart -
What is it I remember?
A time? A place? A person?
Is it from childhood, or another life?
Or does it belong to the future?

Now the sky darkens, and clouds
Like amber-streaked smoke begin
To spread where the conflagration dies away;
In a patch of the palest blue Venus shines,
Lucent and lovely, sending her ancient signal
Across the space of centuries.

1967

To a Stranger in Shadow

I, walking in sunlight down a Dorset lane,
I, and my friend, together making delightful plans -
A Chinese meal, a long laze in the sun, a swim ...
We smile at one another.

Then you, walking in shadow towards us,
Alone and in silence.
But you wear your clothes with an air, and your face
Still bears traces of a far-off beauty.

And yet I know that those dark gloves you wear
Hide hands that have been a long while cold,
And in those clouded eyes that gaze, but do not see,
The August sun is not reflected.
Though skies burn blue and fields are gold,
Grief is your weather.

A wise man told me once that we must have
Something to look forward to, to stay alive,
No matter how absurd or insignificant
(A visit from a friend, a book, a meal, the tail
That wags a welcome, or the blessed peace of bedtime).
Something we must have
If we are to remain alive, he said.

But all your friends are dead, and books
Have lost their meaning.
The meals, not cooked with love, taste sour.
"Dogs are not allowed in this establishment."
And sleep eludes you at the fall of night.

Now, far away, I write these lines
To exorcise your memory from my mind;
I who, walking in sunlight under August skies,
Met with the ghost of you:
Lonely, and far from home.

1968

A song of sorrow for Russia's dead astronauts

After your marvellous journey among the stars
Were you longing for home?
Did you think of your wives and your children as you came
Hurtling back to earth?
Courageous, you travelled far beyond our reach
Discovering, testing, daring.

Now you are gone where even the radio beams
Will never find you.
Hail and farewell, you who were stars
In your own right;
You, who were stars of the space age.

1968

Lines to Beregevoi, Russian astronaut

What more innocent than these? Golden rain and screech
owls, bangers, jumping jacks,
Catherine wheels and sparklers, silver fountains and egyptian
fire...
Crackling bonfire seen with childhood's eye, blazing as
marvellously as Moses' bush...
O Beregevoi, circling the earth tonight in your super-rocket,
Will your discoveries give as much pleasure to so many as
these twinkling toys?

November, 1968

Knowle Mental Hospital

I watched the figures drifting along the paths,
Aimless as autumn's falling leaves.
But these are not mad -
Mad is alive, though raging or mourning - alive!
These people are dead, their eyes
Vacant and shuttered as the windows of wards.

Are these bodies unlived-in? Or are they prisons?
That one, there, under the tree,
To whom does he speak? To a friend
Who once loved him? To God, or his mother?
Or to the self he once was?
Or is he merely murmuring
His anguish to the unlistening sky?

That one, silently plucking her clothes
With bird-thin fingers - what is she trying to grip?
Does she see in her mind's eye
Her husband's hand, a baby's shawl?
Or does she merely cling
To the warmth of wool as to an anchor
In the cold sea where she drifts
And drowns and drowns, but cannot die?

March, 1969

Paul, remembering Stephen

"Here, lad, hold my cloak! - and mine! - and mine!"
Through the still air, like vivid, broken birds,
Hurtle the white and green and scarlet of their outer robes,
Cast off, for easier swing of arms, or to avoid
The splash of the inevitable blood.

I watch, dry-mouthed, myself half-wanting
To appease the insatiable male desire
To aim at things - at anything and if alive,
So much the better...

Alive? Why, this tall target is alive enough!

And yet he stands unmoving in the midst
Of all that wolfish skirmishing, and when
The first stone strikes, he gives a little gasp
Then looks at me and smiles.

(How can a smile knock one off-balance
More than any stone?)

The air begins to whistle round his head,
And yet he makes no effort to protect himself.
His eyes are steadfast on the indifferent sky...
What can he see through all that blood?
What holds his gaze in that blue vacancy?

Then, from his broken mouth the words gush out,
I cannot hear them clearly, but I know
Pain has not forced that torrent from him - only love.

Instantly men become devils, stopping their ears,
Shrieking their hatred, till they drown his voice.
At last the only sound I hear
Is the remorseless thud of stones on naked flesh.

Now he is on his knees; his eyes are closed,
Though the swollen lips move. Gently, gently
He falls and lies like a child asleep.
And I? I cannot stop shaking, though the sun still shines;
For I am no longer my own man. I have taken
The first step down the Damascus Road.

1970

Adam remembers

Eve, I remember the first awakening:
The sun, and a rainbow-hover of wings;
Perfume of lilies crushed for my cradling;
The birds rapt in their first songs,

I remember becoming aware of God -
Not that I saw Him, but the garden shone,
The air hummed with His presence, as I stood
In adoration - I, the first man.

I remember the creatures, gay at His bidding,
Prancing anonymous through the glade
To receive their names from me, or riding
The delirious air above my head.

I remember the last to come - the coils
Shimmering over the grass; the neck curled
Submissive under my hand; the scales
Blazing sapphire, glittering gold.

The marvellous creature, like a blue flame
Flickered among the branches and was gone;
And I, ravished by beauty, for the first time
Knew loneliness, knowing myself alone.

Sleep came then, warm from His hand,
Tenderly, so I went fearless. Now,
Bitterly to the besieged comes day's end,
When the gate yields and the enemy breaks through.

I remember the second awakening: Eve,
You on my breast and the sky seen
Through the bronze web of your hair, my love,
Flesh of my flesh, and bone of my bone;

And then the stealthy rustle, the head
Swaying in sapphire circles in the tree;
The eyes, the lidless eyes that stared
Heart of my heart, at you, at you.

The sky stained with the first cloud;
Birds were mute, even the grass was still;
The first pain stirred deep in my side,
As the apple-blossom began to fall.

I remember seeing the tranquil garden
wake to sunrise for the final time;
I remember our tears... O Eden, Eden,
When will our exile end, and we come home?

1972

A Song for Kate
(to my Mother on her 89th birthday)

The sun, the moon, the stars will shine
For Katie, who is eighty-nine!

Here in this song, I celebrate
The lifetime of my darling Kate.
Red-haired at birth, and thrown aside
(Alas for me, if she had died!),
The tiny Kate showed even then
A dauntless will to live, and when
She'd rested from the shock of birth
She firmly took her place on earth.

The sun, the moon, the stars will shine
For Katie, who is eighty-nine!

And next, a little golden girl
Green-eyed and lissome, every curl
Twinkling with life and energy.
Laughter and tears, sorrow and glee
Coloured her days. The years depart
As mischievous Kate, with loving heart
Dances and sings and sleeps and plays
Into her girlhood's wild-rose days.

The sun, the moon, the stars will shine
For Katie, who is eighty-nine!

Dear Kate, your life has been so long,
To tell it all would make my song,
If I began at morning light,
Last till the sun went down at night!
So bless you - bless you every day,
And please remember what I say:-
I shall expect to find you, Kate,
Waiting for me at Heaven's gate.

The sun, the moon, the stars will shine
For Katie, who is eighty-nine!

1973

Thank you, Tammy

Dear little dog,
You always were the naughty one,
Wilful and noisy - oh, that barking!
But you only had to grin, and all was forgiven...

Everyone loved you, with your silky white fur
And your trim little trot, so all of a piece;
With your gift for relaxing like a child's soft toy.

Dear little dog,
Loving, crafty, mischievous, shy;
A bundle of contrasts yet always consistent.
You cannot have been snuffed out!
Somewhere, your flame still shines.

Though silence greets us now, instead of your shouting,
And only one basket is left by the hearth
Where your old brother lies, puzzled, and grieving,
This song is still a happy one.

Dear little dog,
Thank you for all you gave us.
We shall remember the laughter and loving
And grief is assuaged because you were happy.
Dear little dog, how much we shall miss you.

1975

Desolation

As I was running to the station in the no-man's time
That follows Boxing Day, a shabby car drew up.
An old voice called across the road: "I saw you running -
Would you like a lift?"

One glance at face, and overcoat, and hat, all grey,
Told me that he was genuine. Grateful, I clambered in -
"How kind of you to stop. I hope this won't delay you on
your way?"

"I ain't a-going nowhere, love. You see, I lost my wife
On Christmas Eve, and now I'm driving round
To try and put it all behind me." There I sat,
And mouthed the usual words, rigid with sympathy
and the sheer inadequacy of my remarks.
He sighed and then,
"That's life," he said, squaring his stubble chin,
"That's life."

Oh no, my brave old man, that's death.

1975

Dream tiger

Once he was always awake -
A silent presence on the dark house
Behind the unlocked doors.
Terror, lest he break through,
Convulsed my dreams.

Now he sleeps. Occasionally
He stirs, stretching a gentle paw.
The claws are always sheathed,
And the marvellous eyes relax
In a golden wink.

1990

The Visitor

Against the darkness of the dreaming wood,
Lit by the sunrise, glimmered his single horn,
Fetlock-deep in daffodils he stood,
Silent as snow, the peerless Unicorn.

He was my heart's desire, yet I fled;
Turning my back on him I wept because
Such love and longing mingled with my dread,
So beautiful; so beautiful he was.

All day I hid, until the storm was passed,
Darkness had fallen and the hour was late,
But when I came in sight of home at last,
The unicorn was standing at my gate.

In majesty he stood, and gazed at me;
Beautiful, and compassionate, and wise,
And glinting in the moonlight, I could see
The slow tears falling from his shadowy eyes.

All terror gone, I reached to stroke his mane,
Touching the pearly horn with perfect trust.
Then, knowing I would not see his like again,
I knelt for his forgiveness in the dust.

1990